Troll Teacher Time Savers

Reading & Thinking

Reproducible Activity Sheets for Grades K-1

Troll Associates

Published by Troll Associates, an imprint and registered trademark of Troll Communications L.L.C.

Printed in the United States of America

10 9 8 7 6 5 4 3 2 1

Troll Teacher Time Savers provide a quick source of self-contained lessons and practice material, designed to be used as full-scale lessons or to make productive use of those precious extra minutes that sometimes turn up in the day's schedule.

Troll Teacher Time Savers can help you to prepare a made-to-order program for your students. Select the sequence of Time Savers that will meet your students' needs, and make as many photocopies of each page as you require. Since Time Savers include progressive levels of complexity and difficulty in each book, it is possible to individualize instruction, matching the needs of each student.

Those who need extra practice and reinforcement for catching up in their skills can benefit from Troll Teacher Time Savers, while other students can use Time Savers for enrichment or as a refresher for skills in which they haven't had recent practice. Time Savers can also be used to diagnose a student's knowledge and skills level, in order to see where extra practice is needed.

Time Savers can be used as homework assignments, classroom or small-group activities, shared learning with partners, or practice for standardized testing. See "Answer Key & Skills Index" to find the specific skill featured in each activity.

ANSWER KEY & SKILLS INDEX

Page 1, **Garden Fun:** seed packets; watering can; garden fork; hoe; hose; rake. **(categorizing)**

Page 2, **My Fruit Basket: (categorizing)**

Page 3, **Keep It Cold:** soda; butter; eggs; grapes; steak; milk. **(categorizing)**

Page 4, **Round & Round: (shapes)**

Page 5, **Rolling Along: (similarities/differences)**

Page 6, **Flying High: (similarities/differences)**

Page 7, **Play Ball: (shapes)**

Page 8, **Odd Man Out:** broom; birthday cake; turtle. **(categorizing)**

Page 9, **Who Belongs?:** beetle; turtle; duck; mouse. **(categorizing)**

Page 10, **Fashion Show:** dress; shirt; jeans; high heels. **(categorizing)**

Page 11, **Going Places:** rowboat; submarine; boat, sailboat, raft. **(categorizing)**

Page 12, **Imagine That!: (categorizing)**

Page 13, **Match Mates:** shoe and lace; ball and bat; paint and brush; needle and thread; toothpaste and toothbrush. **(matching)**

Page 14, **Match Ups:** tennis ball and racket; salt and pepper shaker; hammer and nails; needles and yarn; comb and brush. **(matching)**

Page 15, **Super Snacks:** top to bottom, bone; cheese, carrot, acorn. **(categorizing)**

Page 16, **Happy Birthday: (categorizing)**

Page 17, **A Boy and a Pony: (categorizing)**

Page 18, **Run, Run, Run: (categorizing)**

Page 19, **Yum, Yum: (categorizing)**

Page 20, **Surf's Up:** tanker; rowboat; whale; saiboat; penguin; surfer; yacht. **(categorizing)**

Page 21, **Bundle Up!:** hat; coat; mittens; boots; earmuffs; muffler. **(categorizing)**

Page 22, **Clean Up Time:** vacuum; mop; dustpan and brush. **(categorizing)**

Page 23, **At the Library:** books; reading circle; librarian; computer; magazines. **(categorizing)**

Page 24, **Post Office Puzzle:** package; stamp; letter; mailbag. **(categorizing)**

Page 25, **Summer Fun:** sailboat; shells; umbrella; bucket; towel; raft. **(categorizing)**

Page 26, **Which Belongs?:** top to bottom, iron; bed; spoon; glove. **(categorizing)**

Page 27, **Let's Keep Fit:** jogging; basketball; jumping rope; lifting weights; swimming; dancing; skiing. **(categorizing)**

Page 28, **Good for You:** oatmeal; fruit; bread; eggs; carrots; milk; fish. **(categorizing)**

Page 29, **Time to Paint:** top-2,1,3; bottom-3,1,2. **(sequencing)**

Page 30, **An Apple a Day:** top-2,3,1; bottom-Answers will vary. **(sequencing)**

Page 31, **Growing Up:** top-2,3,1; bottom-2,3,1. **(sequencing)**

Page 32, **Up & Around:** top-3,2,1; bottom-1,3,2. **(sequencing)**

Page 33, **Let's Have Fun:** top-2,3,1; bottom-1,3,2. **(sequencing)**

Page 34, **One, Two, Three:** 1-3,1,2; 2-3,1,2; 3-3,2,1. **(sequencing)**

Page 35, **Beach Fun:** 1-2,1,3; 2-3,2,1; 3-3,1,2. **(sequencing)**

Page 36, **Flower Power:** top-b,a; bottom-a,b. **(sequencing)**

Page 37, **High & Tall:** top-a,b; bottom-b,a. **(sequencing)**

Page 38, **Around Town:** 1-3,1,2; 2-1,3,2; 3-1,2,3. **(sequencing)**

Page 39, **Fun Time:** 1-3,2,1; 2-1,3,2; 3-1,3,2. **(sequencing)**

Page 40, **Snack Time:** top-a,b; bottom-a,b. **(sequencing)**

Page 41, **Higher & Higher:** 4,1,2,3. **(sequencing)**

Page 42, **Super Scoop:** 3,2,4,1. **(sequencing)**

Page 43, **Falling Leaves:** 1,2,4,3. **(sequencing)**

Page 44, **Roller Coaster Fun:** 2,4,1,3. **(sequencing)**

Page 45, **Bedtime:** 1,4,3,2. **(sequencing)**

Page 46, **Dinner Time:** Answers will vary. **(sequencing)**

Page 47, **Cooling Off:** The water is cool; The sun is hot. **(sentence sequence)**

Page 48, **Animal Friends:** The bird can fly; The pig is fat. **(sentence sequence)**

Page 49, **Big & Little:** The cat is big; The dog is little. **(sentence sequence)**

Page 50, **Look & See:** Look at my book; I see me. **(sentence sequence)**

Page 51, **All About Leah: (reading comprehension)**

Page 52, **All About Sue: (reading comprehension)**

Page 53, **Playtime: (reading comprehension)**

Page 54, **Fun for All: (reading comprehension)**

Page 55, **Come & Play: (word comprehension)**

Page 56, **A Wet Pet: (word comprehension)**

Page 57, **Lost & Found: (word comprehension)**

Page 58, **Get Your Pet:** top to bottom, yes; no; yes. **(understanding pictures)**

Page 59, **Fun for Two:** top to bottom, yes; yes; no. **(understanding pictures)**

Page 60, **A Cat Nap: (reading comprehension)**

Page 61, **Shower Power: (reading comprehension)**

Page 62, **Let's Play:** top to bottom, yes; no; no. **(understanding pictures)**

Page 63, **A Fat Cat: (word comprehension)**

Page 64, **Fun for Billy: (reading comprehension)**

Page 65, **Happy Birthday: (reading comprehension)**

Page 66, **The Dancer:** top to bottom, loves; tired; rest. **(word comprehension)**

Page 67, **Play Ball!:** top to bottom, ball; play; thank. **(word comprehension)**

Page 68, **Leah's Day:** top to bottom, yes; yes; no. **(reading comprehension)**

Page 69, **I Am Hungry!:** top to bottom, no; yes; no. **(reading comprehension)**

Page 70, **A Little Boat:** top to bottom, red; likes; boat. **(word comprehension)**

Page 71, **Funny Sunny:** top to bottom, no; no; yes. **(reading comprehension)**

Page 72, **A Nice Surprise: (reading comprehension)**

Page 73, **Finders Keepers: (reading comprehension)**

Page 74, **Picnic Fun:** top to bottom, picnic; good; rabbit. **(reading comprehension)**

Page 75, **A Good Game:** top to bottom, hops; hard; try. **(reading comprehension)**

Page 76, **Sarah & Tina: (reading comprehension)**

Garden Fun

What things would you use in the garden?
Draw lines from them to the garden.

Name ______________________________ Date ____________________

My Fruit Basket

Cut out all the fruit and glue it in the basket.
Color the fruit and basket.

Name ______________________ **Date** ______________________

Keep It Cold

What things belong in the refrigerator?
Draw lines from them to the refrigerator.

Name ______________________________ **Date** ______________

Round & Round

Color all the things that are circles.

Name ______________________________ **Date** ____________________

Rolling Along

Use your crayons. Color everything that has wheels.

Name ______________________________ **Date** ____________________

Flying High

Use your crayons. Color everything that has wings.

Name ______________________________ **Date** ____________________

Play Ball

Color all the round things red. Color all the long things yellow.

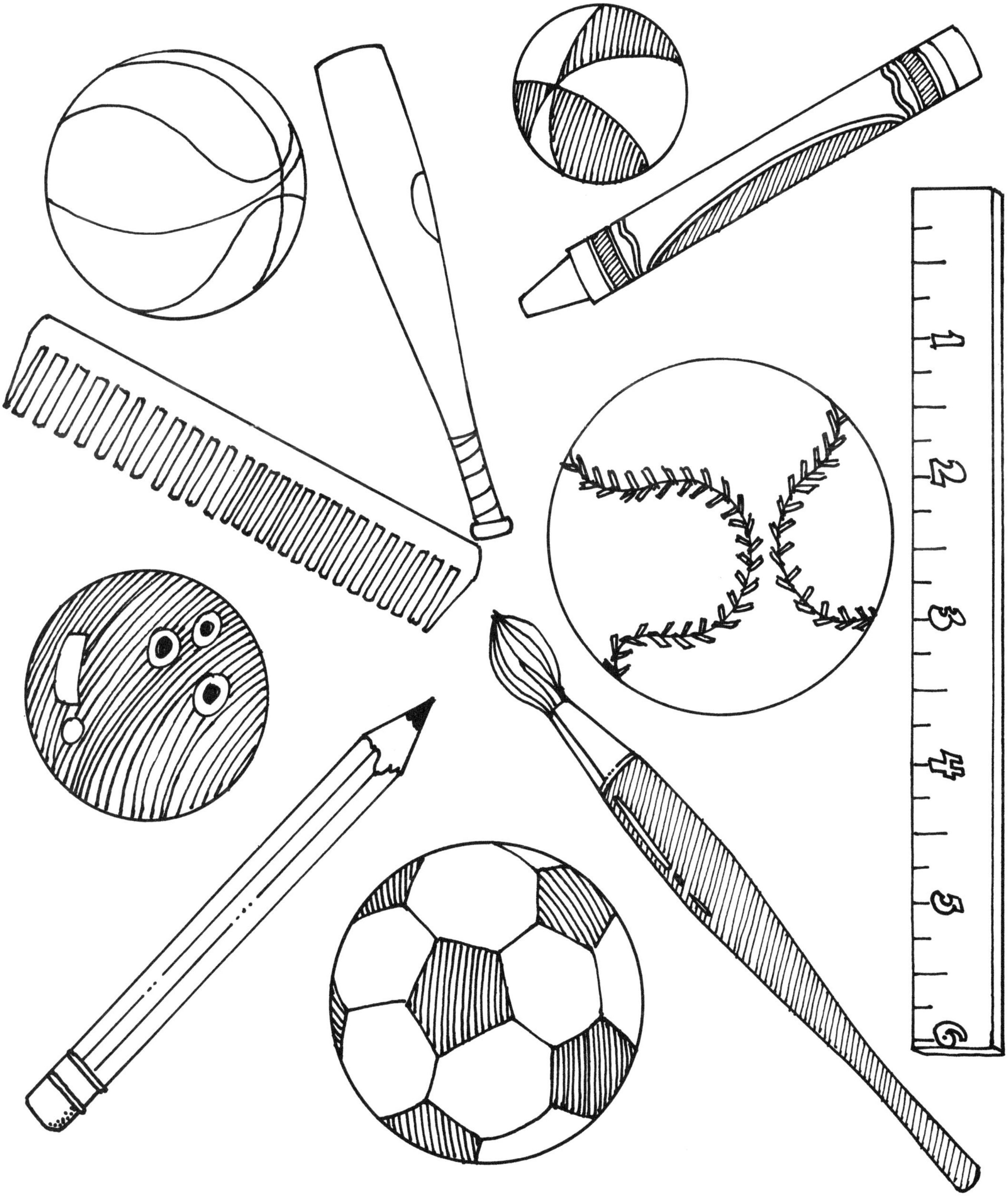

Name ______________________ Date ______________

Odd Man Out

What doesn't belong? Color the thing that is different in each row.

Name ______________________________ **Date** ____________________

Who Belongs?

In each row, one thing does not belong. Cross it out.

Name ______________________________ **Date** ____________________

Fashion Show

What doesn't belong? Color the thing that is different in each row.

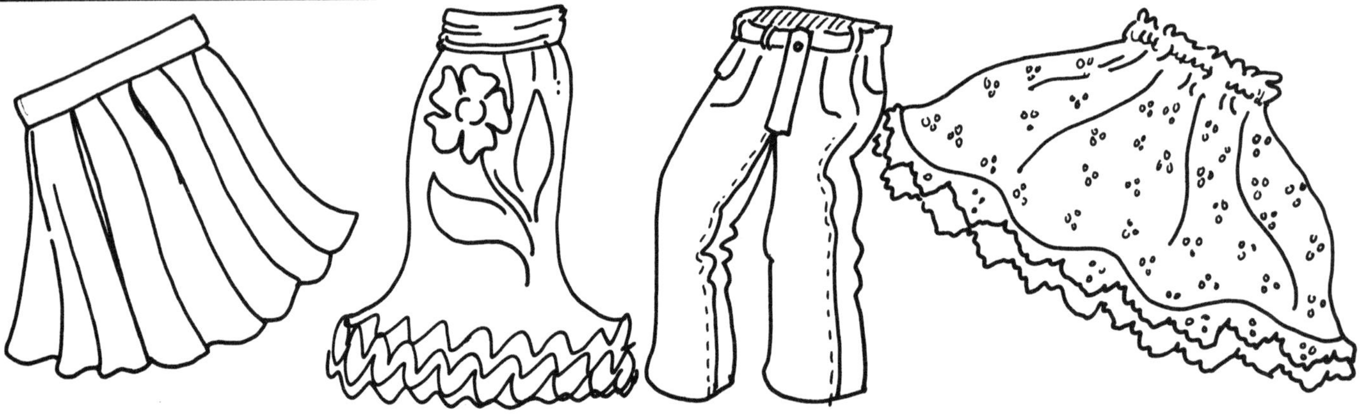

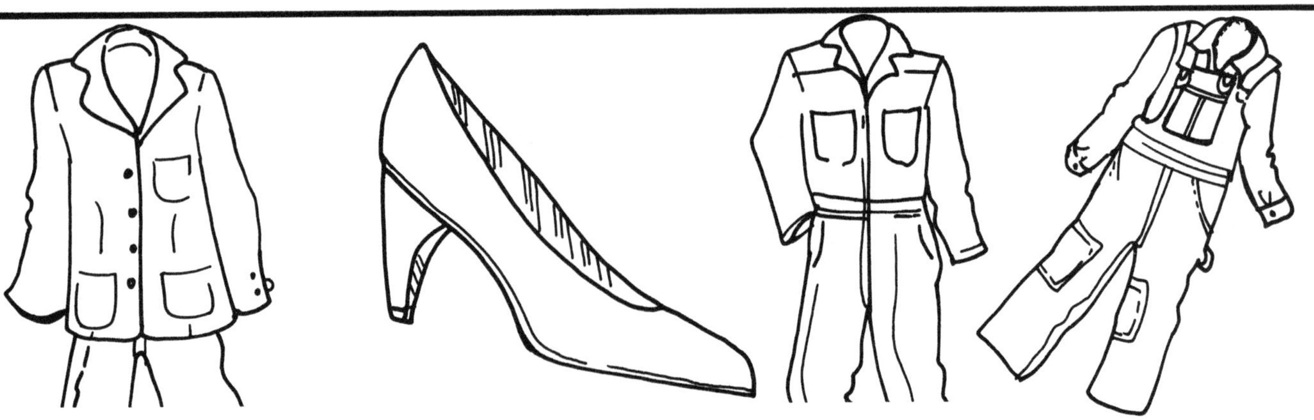

Name________________________________ **Date** ____________________

Going Places

Pretend you want to go to an island in the middle of the ocean. Color the things you could use to get there.

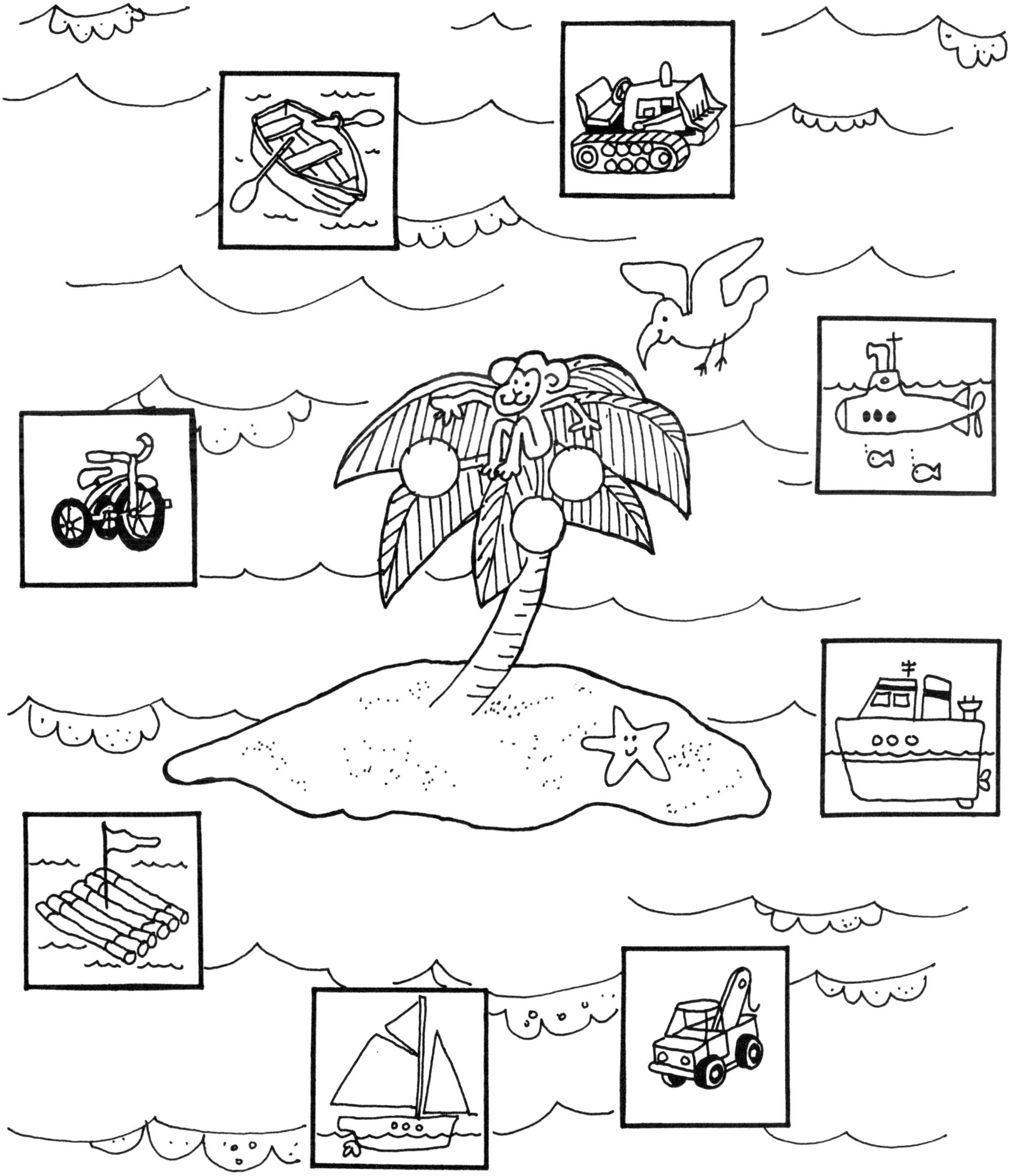

Name ______________________________ **Date** ____________________

Imagine That!

Which animals are make-believe?
Color the make-believe animals purple.

Name ______________________________ **Date** ____________________

Match Mates

Which things go together? Draw lines to join them.

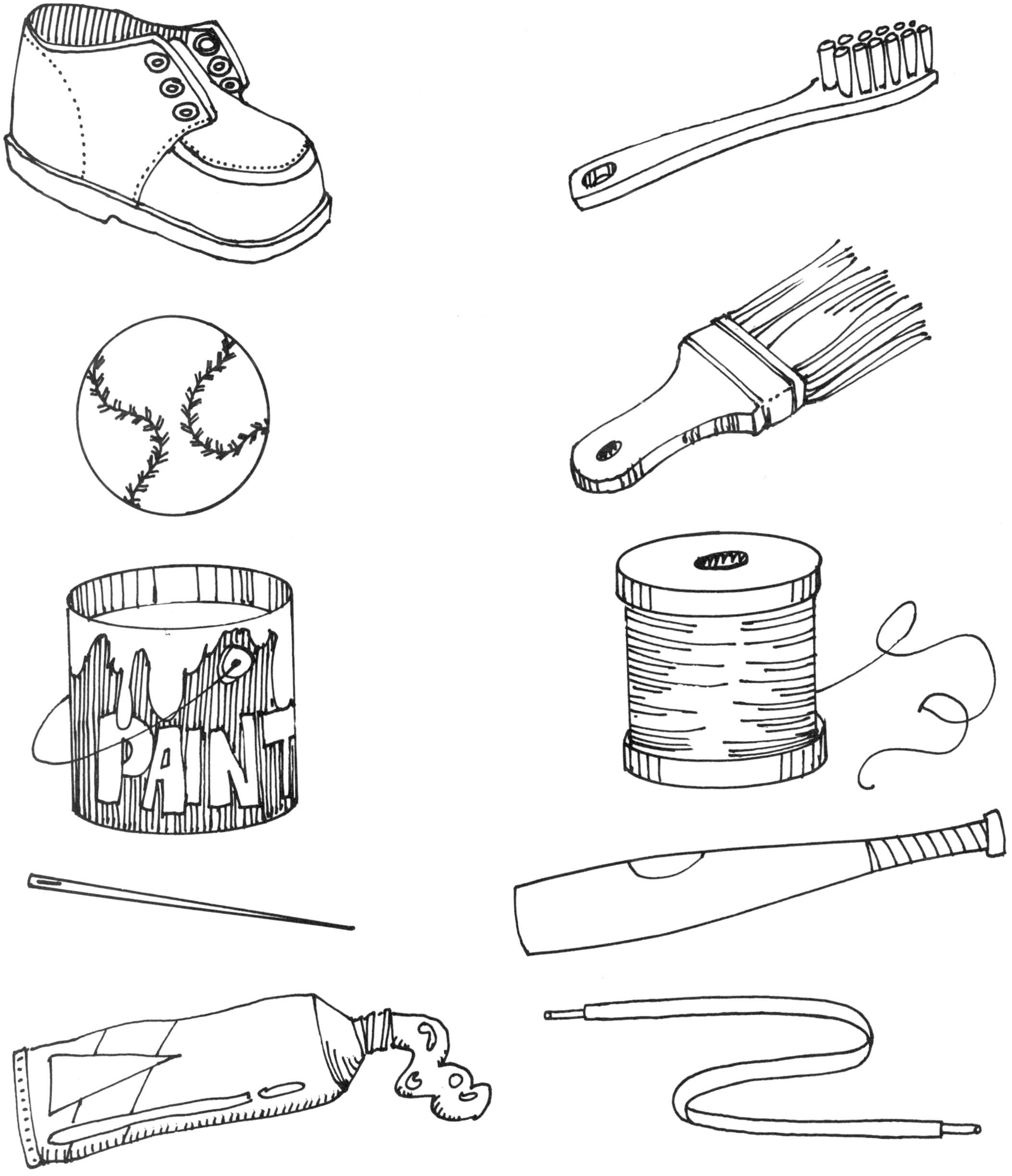

Name ______________________ **Date** ______________________

Match Ups

Which things go together? Draw lines to join them.

Name ______________________ **Date** ______________________

Super Snacks

Which food is each animal's favorite? Color it.

Name ______________________________ **Date** ____________________

Happy Birthday

Color all the things you would find at a birthday party.

Name ______________________________ **Date** ______________________

A Boy and a Pony

Color all the parts of the boy different colors.
Color all the parts of the pony gray.

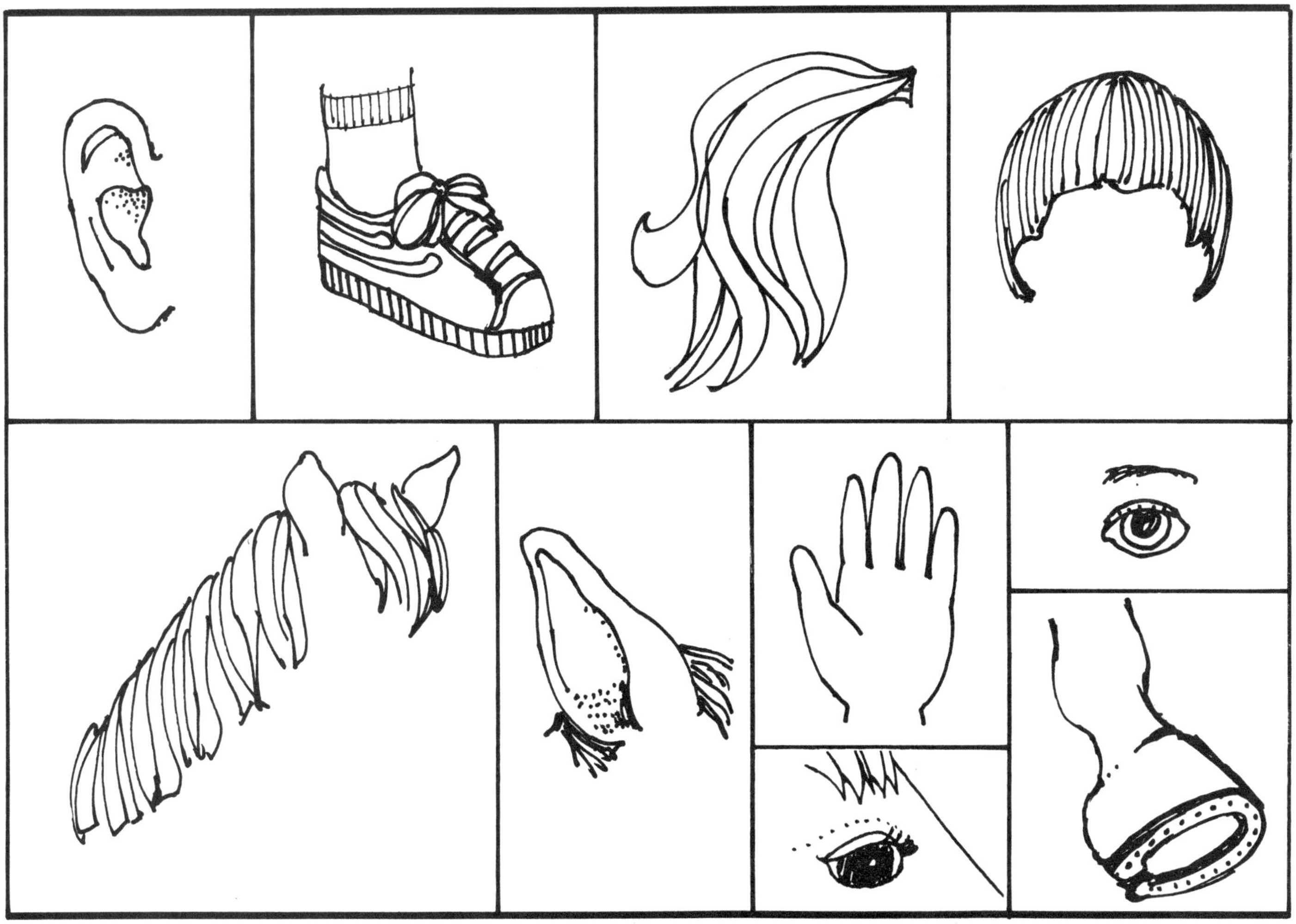

Name ______________________________ **Date** ______________________

Run, Run, Run

Use a yellow crayon to color all the runners wearing letters.
Use a red crayon to color all the runners wearing numbers.

Name ______________________________ **Date** ____________________

Yum, Yum

Color all the things you can eat.

Name ____________________ **Date** ____________________

Surf's Up!

Color all the things you might find on the ocean.

Name ______________________________ **Date** ______________

Bundle Up!

Color all the things you would wear in the cold.

Name ______________________________ **Date** ____________________

Clean Up Time

Color the things we need to clean the house.

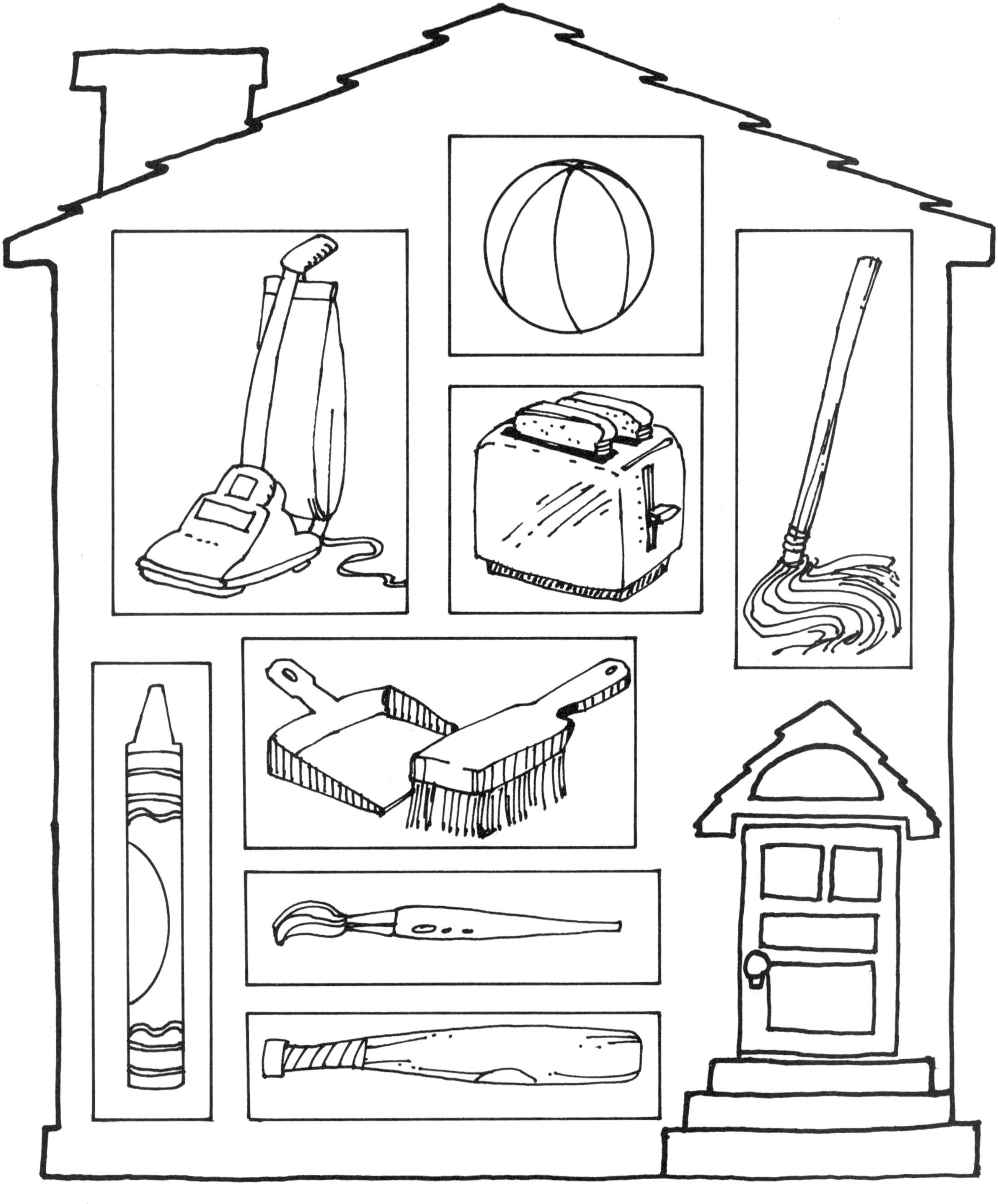

Name ______________________________ **Date** ______________________

At the Library

Draw a line from the library to the things you might find there.

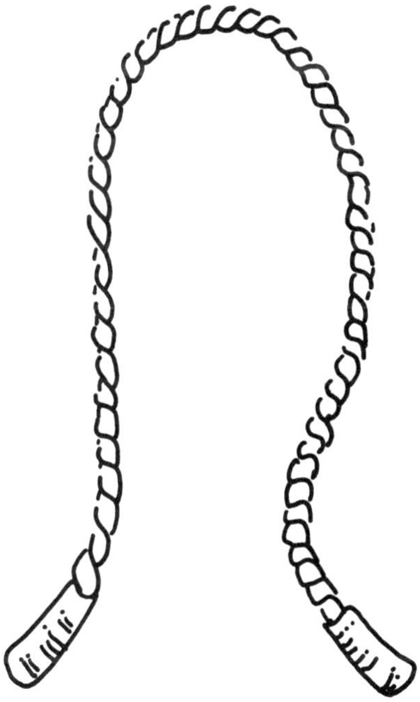

Name ______________________________ **Date** ________________

Post Office Puzzle

Draw a line from the Post Office to the things you might find there.

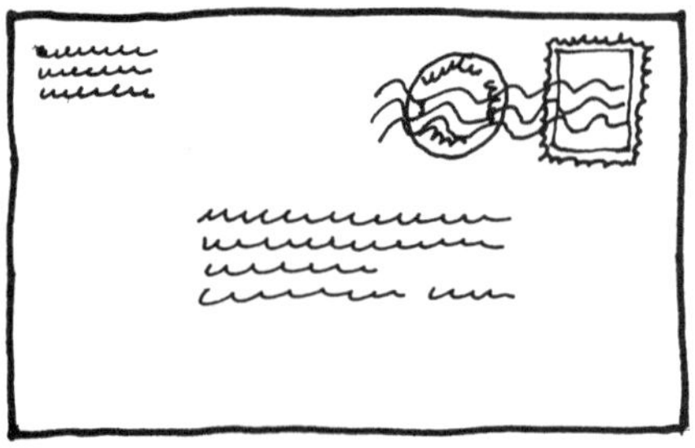

Name ______________________________ **Date** ____________________

Summer Fun

Color all the things you might see at the beach.

Name ______________________________ **Date** ____________________

Which Belongs?

Cross out the item that does not belong in each row.

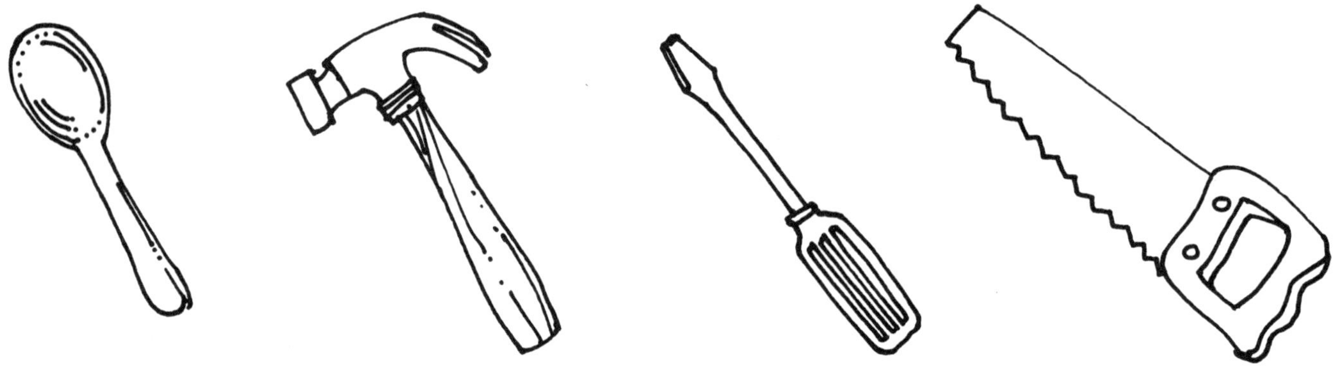

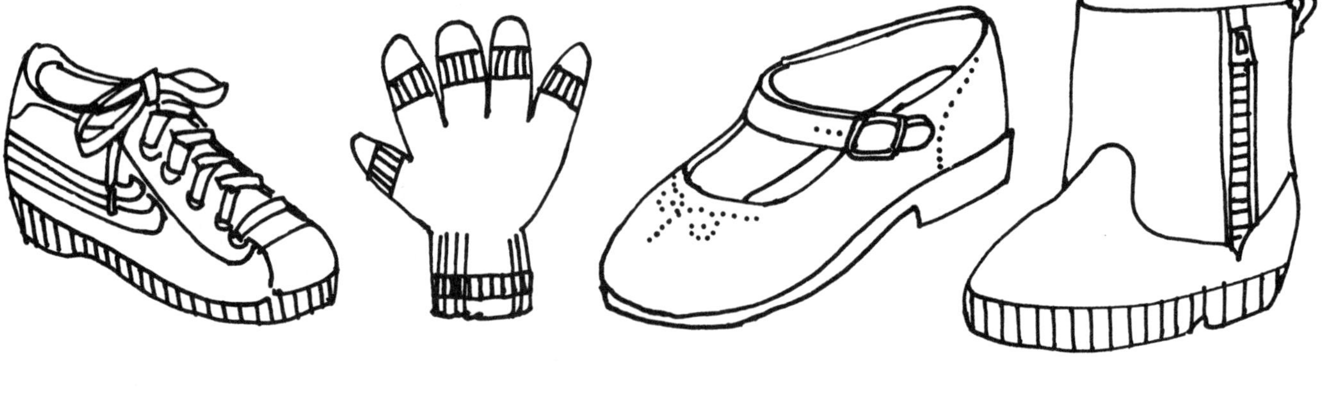

Name ______________________________ **Date** ____________________

Time to Paint

Cut out the pictures in each row. Which picture shows what happened first, next, last? Attach them to another piece of paper in the right order. Don't forget to sign your name.

Cut along dotted lines.

An Apple a Day

Cut out the pictures in each row. Which picture shows what happened first, next, last? Attach them to another piece of paper in the right order. Don't forget to sign your name.

Cut along dotted lines.

Growing Up

Cut out the pictures in each row. Which picture shows what happened first, next, last? Attach them to another piece of paper in the right order. Don't forget to sign your name.

Cut along dotted lines.

Up & Around

Cut out the pictures in each row. Which picture shows what happened first, next, last? Attach them to another piece of paper in the right order. Don't forget to sign your name.

Cut along dotted lines.

Let's Have Fun

Cut out the pictures in each row. Which picture shows what happened first, next, last? Attach them to another piece of paper in the right order. Don't forget to sign your name.

Cut along dotted lines.

One, Two, Three

Look at the pictures in each row. Which comes first? Put 1 in the box. Which comes next? Put 2 in the box. Which comes last? Put 3 in the box.

1.

2.

3.

Name ______________________________ **Date** ____________________

Beach Fun

Look at the pictures in each row. Which comes first? Put 1 in the box. Which comes next? Put 2 in the box. Which comes last? Put 3 in the box.

1.

2.

3.

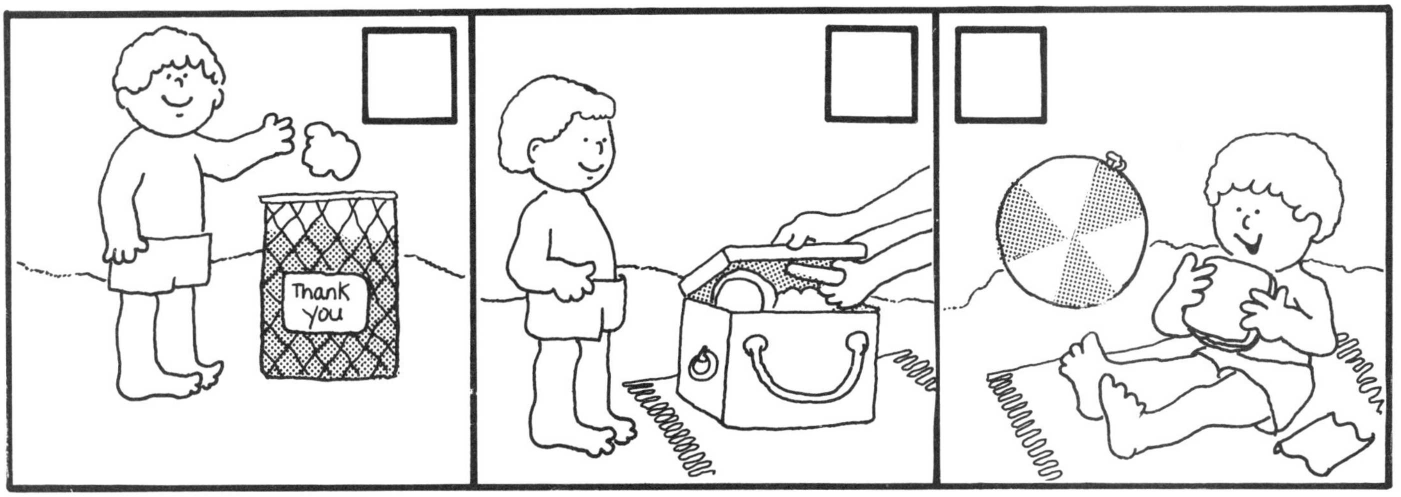

Name ______________________________ **Date** ____________________

Flower Power

Which picture comes BEFORE this one?
Put a B over it.
Which picture comes AFTER this one?
Put an A over it.

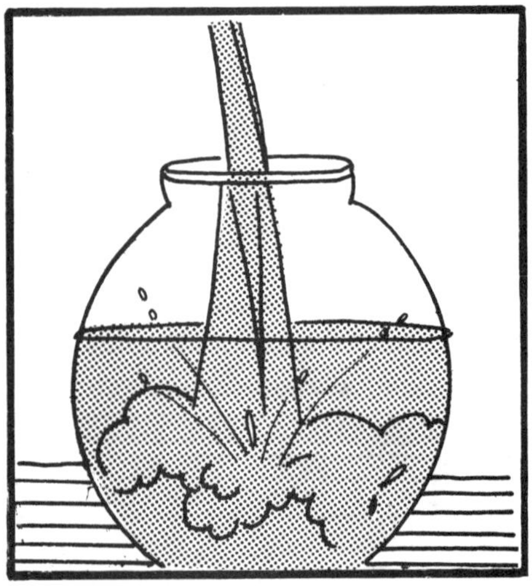

Which picture comes BEFORE this one?
Put a B over it.
Which picture comes AFTER this one?
Put an A over it.

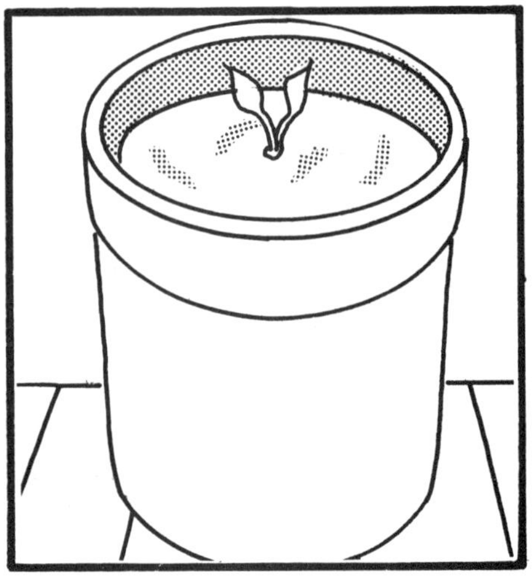

Name ______________________________ **Date** ____________________

High & Tall

Which picture comes BEFORE this one?
Put a B over it.
Which picture comes AFTER this one?
Put an A over it.

Which picture comes BEFORE this one?
Put a B over it.
Which picture comes AFTER this one?
Put an A over it.

Name ______________________ **Date** ______________

Around Town

Look at the pictures in each row. Which comes first? Put 1 in the box. Which comes next? Put 2 in the box. Which comes last? Put 3 in the box.

1.

2.

3.

Name ______________________ **Date** ______________

Fun Time

Look at the pictures in each row. Which comes first? Put 1 in the box. Which comes next? Put 2 in the box. Which comes last? Put 3 in the box.

1.

2.

3.

Name ______________________________ **Date** ____________________

Snack Time

Which picture comes BEFORE this one?
Put a B over it.
Which picture comes AFTER this one?
Put an A over it.

Which picture comes BEFORE this one?
Put a B over it.
Which picture comes AFTER this one?
Put an A over it.

Name ______________________ Date ______________________

Higher & Higher

Look at the pictures. What happens first? Put 1 in the box. What happens next? Put 2 in the box. What happens after that? Put 3 in the box. What happens last? Put 4 in the box.

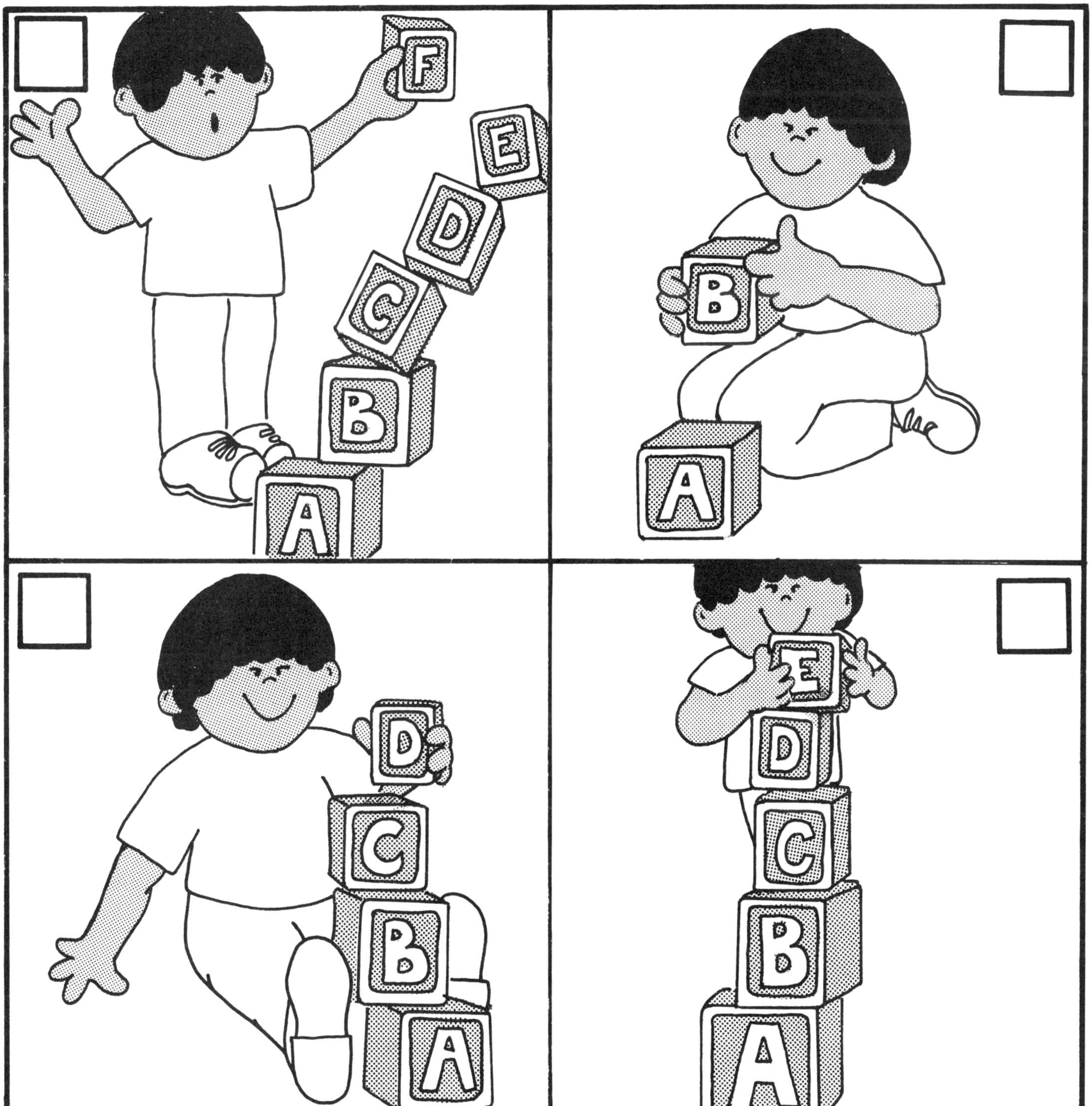

Name ______________________________ **Date** ____________________

Super Scoop

Look at the pictures. What happens first? Put 1 in the box. What happens next? Put 2 in the box. What happens after that? Put 3 in the box. What happens last? Put 4 in the box.

Name ______________________ **Date** ______________

Falling Leaves

Look at the pictures. What happens first? Put 1 in the box. What happens next? Put 2 in the box. What happens after that? Put 3 in the box. What happens last? Put 4 in the box.

Name ______________________ Date ______________________

Roller Coaster Fun

Look at the pictures. What happens first? Put 1 in the box. What happens next? Put 2 in the box. What happens after that? Put 3 in the box. What happens last? Put 4 in the box.

Name ______________________ **Date** ______________________

Bedtime

Look at the pictures. What happens first? Put 1 in the box. What happens next? Put 2 in the box. What happens after that? Put 3 in the box. What happens last? Put 4 in the box.

Name ______________________________ **Date** ____________________

Dinner Time

Look at the pictures. What happens first? Put 1 in the box. What happens next? Put 2 in the box. What happens after that? Put 3 in the box. What happens last? Put 4 in the box.

Name ______________________________ **Date** ____________________

Cooling Off

Look at the picture. Read the words. Write the words to make a sentence about the picture. Then color the picture.

water The cool is

______ ______ ______ ______.

The hot is sun

______ ______ ______ ______.

Name ______________________ **Date** ______________________

Animal Friends

Look at each picture. Read the words. Write the words to make a sentence about the picture. Then color the picture.

fly bird can The

______ ______ ______ ______.

is The fat pig

______ ______ ______ ______.

Name ____________________ **Date** ______________

Big & Little

Look at each picture. Read the words. Write the words to make a sentence about the picture. Then color the picture.

cat is The big

______ ______ ____ ______.

little The is dog

______ ______ ____ ______.

Name ______________________ Date ____________

Look & See

Look at each picture. Read the words. Write the words to make a sentence about the picture. Then color the picture.

at Look book my

____ ____ ____ ____.

I me see

____ ____ ____.

Name ____________ Date ____________

All About Leah

Draw a line from the sentence to the picture it tells about.
Then color the pictures.

This is Leah.

This is Leah's friend.

This is Leah's bike.

Name ______________________________ **Date** ____________________

All About Sue

Draw a line from the sentence to the picture it tells about. Then color the pictures.

Here is Sue's House.

Here is Sue's dog.

Here is Sue's father.

Name ______________________________ **Date** ______________________

Playtime

Draw a line from the sentence to the picture it tells about. Then color the pictures.

We like to jump rope.

We like to play kickball.

We love to play.

Name ________________________________ **Date** ____________________

Fun for All

Draw a line from the sentence to the picture it tells about. Then color the pictures.

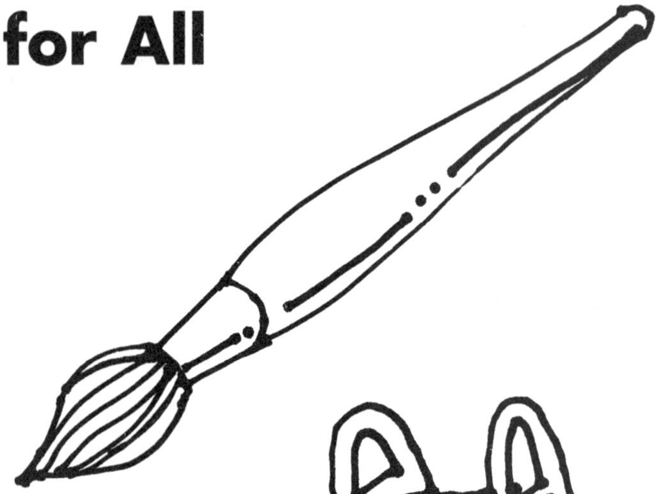

I can run and jump.

You can paint with this.

You can play on this.

Name ______________________________ **Date** ____________________

Come & Play

Color the pictures.
Cut them out.
Put them where
they should go.

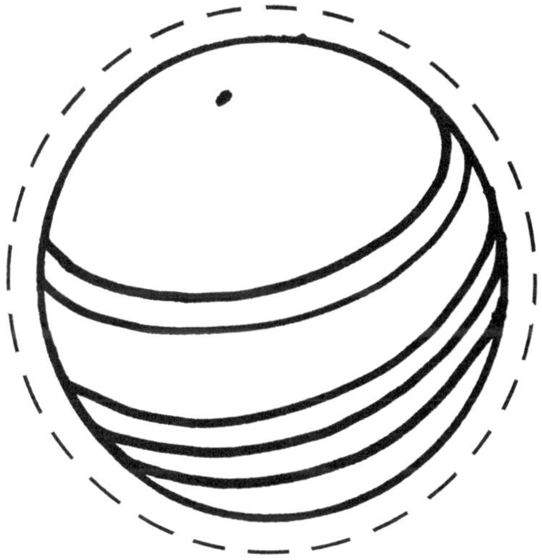

Read the sentences.

The dog wants to play.
The ball is blue.

The ____ wants to play.

The ____ is blue.

Name ____________________ **Date** ____________

A Wet Pet

Color the pictures. Cut them out. Put them where they should go.

Read the sentences. The bike went fast.
My new pet is a fish.

The ______ went fast.

My new pet is a ______.

Name ______________________ **Date** ______________

Lost & Found

Color the pictures. Cut them out.
Put them where they should go.

Read the sentences.

Mike lost his shoe.
He found it in the wagon.

Mike lost his ______________ .

He found it in the ______________ .

Name ______________________________ **Date** ____________________

Get Your Pet

Look at the picture. Then write **yes** or **no**.

This is a pet show. ______

We see two dogs. ______

One pet ran away. ______

Name ______ **Date** ______

Fun for Two

Look at the picture. Then write **yes** or **no**.

Ramon has a bike. ______

Kim can ride. ______

Ramon and Kim are in a car. ______

Name ______ **Date** ______

A Cat Nap

Draw a line from the sentence to the picture it tells about.
Then color the pictures.

Josh has a balloon.

The children had a race.

The kitten went to sleep.

Name ______________________________ **Date** ____________________

Shower Power

Draw a line from the sentence to the picture it tells about. Then color the picture.

Jill sat under the tree to read her book.

Then it began to rain.

Jill got wet on the way home.

Name ______________________________ **Date** ____________________

Let's Play

Look at the picture. Then write **yes** or **no**.

A dog and a cat are in the picture. ______

There are three children in the picture. ______

One boy holds his hat in his hand. ______

Name ______ Date ______

A Fat Cat

Color the pictures. Cut them out.
Put them where they should go.

Read the sentences.

The cat is fat and yellow.
The rocket is ready to fly.

The ______ is fat and yellow.

The ______ is ready to fly.

Name ________________________ **Date** ________________

Fun for Billy

Billy comes to play. He takes a ride on the  .
Up, up he goes. It is fun. Billy likes the .

What does the story tell about? Color the picture that shows.

Name ______________________________ **Date** ____________________

Happy Birthday

It is Jane's birthday.
Father will make a cake.
Jane wants to help.
Father says she can.

What does the story tell about? Color the picture that shows.

Name ____________________ Date ____________________

The Dancer

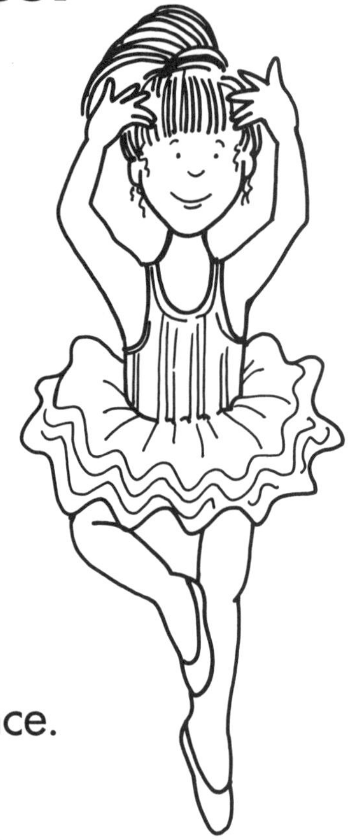

Maria loves to dance.
She dances all night long.
Now she is tired.
Time to rest.

Write the word that goes in each sentence.

Maria ______________ to dance.

She is ______________.

Maria has to ______________.

rest loves tired

Name ______________________ Date ______________

Play Ball!

Juan has a new ball.
He lets all the
children play with it.
They run around.
They play and play.
They all thank Juan.

Write the word that goes in each sentence.

Juan has a _______________ .

Juan lets the children _______________ with it.

The children _______________ Juan.

ball **thank** **play**

Name _______________ **Date** _______________

Leah's Day

It is Leah's birthday today. She is having a party. All her friends are coming. They will have fun.

Write **yes** or **no** in the spaces below.

Leah is having a party. ______

She is happy. ______

Her friends will not be there. ______

Name ______ **Date** ______

I Am Hungry!

Tony wants to eat.
He wants to eat cake
and ice cream and candy.
Tony eats and eats.
Then he feels sick.

Write **yes** or **no** in the spaces below. Then color Tony.

Tony wants to watch TV.

Tony wants ice cream.

Tony feels fine.

Name ______________________ **Date** ______________

A Little Boat

Andy has a little red car.
Lisa has a little boat.
Lisa likes Andy's red car.
So she paints her boat red.

Write the word that goes in each sentence.

Andy's car is ________________.

Lisa ________________ Andy's car.

Lisa paints her ________________ red.

likes boat red

Name ______________________ Date ______________

Funny Sunny

Here comes Sunny.
He is a big dog.
He can jump.
Ask him to sit
and he sits.
Sunny is a good pet.

Write **yes** or **no**. Then color Sunny.

Sunny is a big goat. ____________

Ask him to sit and he jumps. ____________

Sunny is a good pet. ____________

Name ____________________ **Date** ____________

A Nice Surprise

"I have a surprise for you," says Josh.
"I am holding it behind my back."
"It's a balloon," says Cindy.
"How did you guess?" asks Josh.

What does the story tell about? Color the picture that shows.

Name ______________________________ **Date** ____________________

Finders Keepers

The girls and boys were playing ball. The ball got lost in the grass. The girls and boys looked and looked. At last they found the ball. They found a penny and a toy airplane, too.

What does the story tell about? Color the picture that shows.

Name ______________________________ **Date** ____________________

Picnic Fun

The children go on a picnic. They eat many good things. They take a walk and see a rabbit. They play some games. Soon it will be time to go home.

Write the word that goes in each sentence.

The children go on a ________.

They eat ________ things.

They see a ________.

rabbit good picnic

Name ____________ **Date** ____________

A Good Game

Kim shows John a new game. She makes some boxes. Then she hops in them. John says it looks hard. He hops. He misses the box. But he will try again.

Write the word that goes in each sentence.

Kim ______________ in the boxes.

John says it looks ______________ .

John will ______________ again.

hard **try** **hops**

Name ______________ Date ______________

Sarah & Tina

Sarah wants to play dolls. Tina says no. Sarah cannot play with Tina's dolls. Sarah gets mad and goes home.

What does the story tell about? Color the picture that shows.

Name ____________________ Date ________________